Tracy's Story—
The Other Side of the Coin

Tracy Lynn Armstrong

MILVERSTEAD PUBLISHING

Philadelphia

ISBN-13: 978-0-9842847-4-0
ISBN-10: 0-9842847-4-0

Cover and interior designed by Joel Friedlander
www.TheBookDesigner.com
Foreword edited by Heather Goodman

Milverstead Publishing, LLC
31 Rampart Drive
Chesterbrook, PA 19087
(484)653-6205

Visit us on the web!
http://www.milversteadpublishing.com

Foreword

Tracy, our darling daughter. A happy, perfect, chubby baby girl. Our gift from heaven, born in 1964.

With each passing month, we noticed she was not progressing like our son had. Tracy was not sitting or crawling, and her legs were wobbly. After a visit to our pediatrician, the journey began. It took us to Duke Hospital and the Mayo Clinic. At seven months old our daughter was diagnosed with Spinal Muscular Atrophy (SMA).

In 1965, little was known about SMA. There was only one paragraph about the disease in most medical books, and most pediatricians had never seen a child with this condition. We were told our daughter would die within the first five years of her life. Needless to say, our world was crushed.

Tracy was brave, more so than me. She always wanted to go down the largest slide at the park. Her dad picked her up from her wheelchair, climbed the steps with her in his arms, and down the slide they flew. I was so frightened that I walked across the park while they were being adventurous. Tracy and her dad always laughed at me for not believing in them!

I have always been very proud that Richard is such a big part of all our lives, especially when it comes to the children. Having leaned on one another during times of despair and joy, we will be celebrating our forty-ninth anniversary this year.

It hasn't always been easy. Richard and I have faced many hardships: dividing time between our three children, meeting financial needs, and making time for our marriage. Though we both worked out of necessity, our health insurance was canceled when Tracy was a year old because the company claimed SMA was a pre-existing disease. Another two years and many medical bills later, Richard changed jobs to work for UPS, and Tracy was again covered. Richard worked nights, and I worked days so one of us would be home most of the time.

Richard drove a tractor trailer for UPS and left for work around 1:00 a.m. During the night, I turned Tracy and suctioned her lungs free of fluid. On weekends, Richard did this, which allowed me to sleep through the night. When she called us with her high-pitched, little voice during the night, she would say thank you and, "I am sorry I had to call you." We always told her she did not need to be sorry; we did not mind whatsoever. We both were so humbled by this.

Tracy was in and out of hospitals many times a year. Our sadness continued as Tracy lost control of muscles that allowed her to perform even the simplest tasks. At four years old, she could no longer roll over in bed. At five, after a month-long stay in the hospital with a collapsed lung, she lost the ability to move her arms to her face. She struggled with processes that most of us take for granted: breathing, swallowing, and handling her own secretions.

As years went by, Tracy began choking nearly all of the time. The doctor told us to purchase a suction machine, which included tubing to be inserted down her throat. When Tracy was nine years old, she decided she could suction herself and insisted upon performing this life saving treatment on her own. This was the beginning of our learning to trust her judgment concerning her medical well-being. Her dad and I became her assistants. Soon her brother and sister became her assistants.

Tracy and her siblings brought great delight to one another. Her older brother Ricky carried Tracy all over. From the time she was four until she was about eight, Ricky put her on a blanket and pulled her on it from place to place. They played Pac-Man and other computer games. When Tracy's younger sister Wendy got old enough, the three of them played board games and cards, with Tracy using a card holder. The three children performed plays for the adults, and it seemed like Tracy always played the part of a horse because of her reclining wheelchair, which the children draped with sheets. If the children played school, Tracy was always the teacher. Ricky and Tracy were pals as little children, and as older children do, he grew up and left home. But God had blessed Tracy with a younger sister. When Wendy got her driver's license, the two sisters went to the mall to window shop.

In their teens, the girls ran a button business for which they designed and personalized large buttons they sold for a dollar. Wendy and Tracy went to the movies, ate at Italian restaurants, and shared all the things sisters do.

Alone time was spent with books on tape, indexing Tracy's massive collection of music tapes, or running her in-home banking business. If anyone in the family needed a quick five dollars before allowance or pay day, Tracy lent it to us. Of course, we had to sign loan papers and pay back a prorated amount of a fixed interest. Tracy also loved playing with her pets. I had read somewhere that garden snakes were excellent pets for disabled children. I purchased a baby green garden snake for Tracy. She loved the little snake and asked me to sit the cage on her tray, so she could watch the snake for hours. Sometimes her daddy got it out and let it wrap around her arms. Sunshine, a yellowish kitten, slept with Tracy, sat on her lap, and attended homebound school with her.

The local public school system provided Tracy with her homebound education. Every year prior to Christmas, Tracy and I planned a lunch menu for the principal, secretary, and homebound teacher. We chose placemats and tablecloths, and with Tracy reading the recipe to me, we prepared the meal together. Several different years her classes came to visit.

Our home became the place to be. During the summer, kids swam in the pool while Tracy lay on a float with a life jacket on or in the arms of her friends who pulled her around the pool. Richard and I were so grateful for these wonderful young people. They provided something we could not: friendship, buddies, and the special relationships teens have with their peers.

Medically, we experienced highs and lows. When Tracy was eleven, we returned to Duke Hospital. I had thought perhaps the doctors had made a mistake since Tracy had already far exceeded her five-year life expectancy. The follow-up revealed there was no mistake. We attributed her longer-than-expected life to her positive outlook and quick and excellent care, though there were no real concrete answers when so many children with SMA did not make it.

When Tracy was thirteen, we were vacationing at Myrtle Beach. At a restaurant she choked and turned blue. We struggled to put our fingers down her throat to remove the piece of food that was choking her. After retrieving the piece of fish, Tracy was exhausted and weak. The restaurant called an ambulance. At the hospital, the doctor ordered an IV to replenish her fluids. After a nurse tried several times to find a good vein, a young doctor came in and felt sure he had located the vein he could use. Tracy told him, "That vein is not good." He insisted, and as he patted the vein, Tracy asked, "How sure are you? Let's make a bet!"

The young doctor said, "I will bet you everything I have in my pocket." He tried hard to insert the needle into the vein, but as soon as he accomplished the task, the vein collapsed. Through tears, Tracy said, "Pay up, and I will tell you which vein to use." With an embarrassed look, he emptied his pockets of change and dollar bills onto the bed. Tracy proceeded to tell him which vein was good, and he inserted the needle without a problem. Tracy left the hospital the next day $1.68 richer, and her purpose was served. We always told her she was not alive without purpose. She felt she had a mission in life, to educate, share and council.

Richard and I knew we had to toughen Tracy to face the curiosity of the world, the questions asked of her. We wanted her to realize she was of value, that she was needed. Tracy talked to everyone. She was witty and funny and had a way of making people comfortable.

Strangers often talked about Tracy over her head instead of directly to her. I would say, "Tracy, why don't you answer this question?" Some people patted her on the head, and she said she felt like a dog. She wanted to "bark," especially when she was in her late teens. We barked together and laughed once we were alone again. The most popular question was, "What is wrong with the poor little thing?" This was my beautiful daughter they were speaking about; if Tracy heard the word "thing," she rarely said a word. But she soon learned to speak up and say, "Oh, I have Progressive Muscular Spinal Atrophy, Werdnig-Hoffmann Disease." She was open, quick, and ready to explain or converse on any subject, including SMA.

In high school, Tracy was accepted into the Honor Society, and she joined many field trips. When her senior prom arrived, her dad was her date. Tracy was so proud, all dressed up in her royal blue satin evening grown with a thick sash and scooped neck. Her dad picked her up from her wheelchair and danced with her. During other dances, she used her electric wheelchair and went from side to side and in circles. She was surrounded by her peers, and it truly was a magical night.

Graduation day. I remember watching Tracy on the football field as a bee circled her face. She was unable to wave it away, and it finally stung her. Her head fell backwards, and I almost jumped out of the bleachers to run to her, but our family members told me "No," that it would embarrass her in front of her peers. For once I listened, and a fellow student pushed her head back into place. Another lesson Mom learned: trust that Tracy could and would handle herself. Later, when I told her what I almost did, Tracy laughed. "Mom, you raised me to think for myself. Did you not believe I would ask for help?"

At the age of 17, Tracy was blooming into a beautiful young lady. She decided she would write a book for two reasons. First, she wanted to write to the parents who were given special angels, and second, to write to SMA children who needed advice on dealing with daily challenges. She wrote everything she knew related to her disease, although she never met another child with SMA. This was the inspiration for Tracy's story, *The Other Side of the Coin*. Each page was a struggle, for she used a pencil to hit the electric typewriter, letter by letter while lying in a reclining wheelchair. She continued working on her manuscript until a few days prior to her death.

In addition to her writing, Tracy addressed local colleges and church youth groups about what it was like being handicapped and about her faith and acceptance of death and dying. She also reigned as Junior Miss Wheelchair of North Carolina and MDA Poster Child for the Southern Piedmont area. Tracy desired to do so much more, but time and strength ran short. Her five-year life expectancy had turned into twenty-five-years. Tracy's battle with SMA ended October 19, 1989.

Tracy always had a lot of concern for us as her parents. As she aged and knew death was approaching, she wanted to know that we were okay. She began to prepare us. When Richard, Tracy, and I attended a funeral for a childhood friend who died of cancer, Tracy decided to plan her own funeral and write her will. She divided up her assets: music collection to her brother, jewelry and doll collection to her sister. Tracy wanted a celebration of life at her funeral: the youth band from church, "Dancing on the Ceiling" by Lionel Richie, yellow roses (not red because red was too depressing), and hundreds of multi-colored balloons released in the courtyard. She said, "Mom, don't cry. Be happy because I will be in Heaven, walking and dancing. And no more pain or suction machines." I made those promises but cried myself to sleep that night.

The event that changed everything. Tracy was in the hospital; her dad was holding her in his arms when she stopped breathing. I quickly called the nurse, and they resuscitated her, so she could start breathing again. After leaving the hospital, Tracy told me that when she stopped breathing she was in the corner of the room. She felt no pain and wanted to go to Heaven, but when she saw both of her parents crying, she could not leave us, so she started breathing again. I cannot express the chills that ran over me and the fight I had to keep tears from coming. I managed, by the grace of God, to tell her we would never allow her to be resuscitated again.

During the weeks after that particular hospital visit, Tracy wanted a living will. With paper and pen she dictated her wishes. No life support, no resuscitation, no trache. She said, "Mom, I am so tired. Please do not cry. I am ready for Heaven." I realized she wanted permission to die, so we made an agreement. When it appeared it was her time to go, I would sing her favorite song to tell her we were okay, and she could stop fighting for life.

On October 18, 1989, Tracy was in the hospital with pneumonia, receiving breathing treatments several times a day. The lung specialist and pediatric physician told me they had done all they could, that she was drowning in her own fluids. Tracy made sure her wonderful doctor of twenty-five years put her living will on her chart. She weighed thirty-two pounds.

11

That night, Tracy and I talked and laughed. She called her friends. I realize now, she was saying goodbye.

Richard was asleep at home since he would leave the house at 12:30 a.m. to go to work. Our other daughter was pregnant with twins and at home with her family, and our son was at home with his family. By 11:00 p.m., Tracy had just finished her breathing treatment, and she was beginning to struggle once again. She told me she needed another round. The nurses came back and told us they could not give another treatment so soon. The doctor was called at home, and we talked. I quickly called Richard and told him to come to the hospital. He was in a daze and kept asking, "Are you sure?" We'd had so many close calls over the years, and like a miracle, Tracy always bounced back. By midnight, I called Barbara, a close friend, requesting she call the priest. The phone rang, and it was Diane, another close friend to Tracy. She came to the hospital, and with all of us there together, Tracy had her last rites. We prayed and sang Tracy's favorite song. After we kissed her and told her we loved her, she asked, "Are you all okay?" When I assured her we were, she made her last request to us. "Mommy and Daddy kiss each other and tell each other you love one another." Tracy passed away at 1:09 a.m. with us singing and holding her hands.

My heart actually hurt; I was in pain. I kept my word to her and followed all her instructions. I wanted to hold on to her, but I kept thinking about the corner of the room. I loved her more than my own pain, so we released her to God, and thanked God for giving us the honor of having Tracy for twenty-five years.

Tracy was wonderful, quick-minded, and had a sense of humor that was a blessing to us and to everyone she met along our journey. Tracy's friends wanted to express the inspiration she was to them; their comments have been included at the end of the book.

We loved her, protected her, and gave her fight when she needed it. In return, she gave us love, advice, laughter, and taught us about acceptance, strength, and to be fearless as we dealt with life.

We complete her dream now by publishing her manuscript; peace and closure have engulfed me as we go to press.

Thank you, Milverstead Publishing and Chris Finlan, for guiding us through publication to complete Tracy's dream.

Also, huge thanks to Heather Goodman, my foreword editor.

Helen Baldwin, you are an angel. Thank you for retyping Tracy's manuscript.

Janice Armstrong
February, 2010

Special Note

Several years after I wrote my own book about our baby Jeffrey's brief earthly stay (also courtesy of SMA), I met Janice online, thrilled to learn we lived fairly close to each other! Janice was kind enough to send a copy of Tracy's book so I could read it; by the time I finished, I felt like I'd had met Tracy. The Armstrongs and I have kept up through the years (though we still have yet to meet in person), and I am delighted to be a small part of this heartfelt project.

Thanks to a generous dose of angel intervention, both of our books are now in the hands of Milverstead Publishing LLC, founded by Christopher Finlan. Chris' novel, *Not A Fire Exit*, based loosely on an SMA family he knows, came to my attention near the end of 2009, just as my latest (stalled) book revision should have been making its own waves. Once I joined the Milverstead team, I 'happened' to learn that Richard and Janice were ready to publish Tracy's book. They, too, signed up for Milverstead immediately.

Tracy's book needed to be retyped for Joel, the book designer. Since Janice was unable to do it herself because of health concerns, I was asked if I'd like to do it. It has been my pleasure.

After having just fretted over each minute detail in my own book for its reissue, I yearned to correct some of Tracy's spelling, grammar, and punctuation. It was almost painful for this perfectionist wannabe to ignore the variety of minor goofs which I could have so easily fixed... until I visualized Tracy reclined in her wheelchair, patiently typing out each letter of her beloved book with a pencil eraser, daunting deliberation and determination, and the sheer joy with which she graced those she met... expending energy that was increasingly difficult to harness.

That image squelched any further desire to 'perfect' Tracy's writing.

Because it's already perfect. It's Tracy.

Helen Baldwin
The Jeffrey Journey

Tracy's Story—

The Other Side of the Coin

"Mommie, when I go to heaven, I'm going to have a wheelchair with wings".

That's what a blond hair, pig tailed, freckled face, little 5 year old girl told her Mother about 17 years ago. I know because I am that little girl.

Everyone always said I was someone special, but I always thought I was pretty ordinary except for being handicapped.

I did all the normal things that thousands of other kids did. I went to kindergarten, I was a Girl Scout, I went to Camp, but I guess I did do something's a little differently. It's like that old adage— there's more then one way to skin a cat, and I've lived by that my entire life.

Kindergarten

§

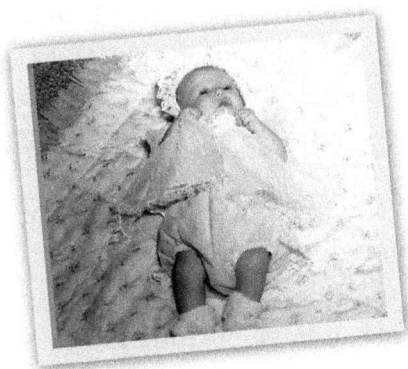

I really enjoyed kindergarten! When my Mother started looking for a day care for my sister and I, she had a lot of trouble as soon as she told them I was in a wheelchair. They said "No", but when Mom went to Mrs. Blythe's "Little Peoples School", she explained all about me and asked if it was okay?

Mrs. Blythe said "of course, why wouldn't it be?" She never gave it a second thought, I was just another kid.

There were times when I could not go outside with the other kids because I had a cold or the weather was too bad. When I had to stay in, Mrs. Blythe made me feel real special. She had this special game she kept in the kitchen cabinet, it was a board with colored pegs that you made pictures with. She wouldn't let the other kids play with it... no one but me, so I really didn't mind staying in.

I remember only once getting in trouble in kindergarten, it doesn't seem very important now, but then... it seemed terrible...

It was during rest period. I was suppose to be asleep, but instead I was looking around the room,

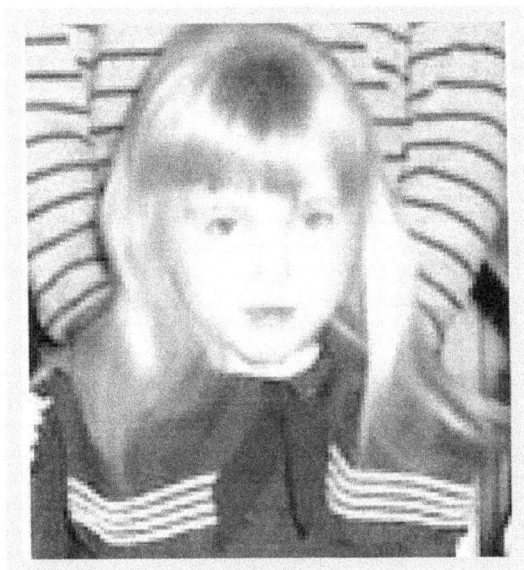

and then I spotted a toy on the shelf about six feet away, and I decided to get it. I rolled a lot as a baby, but by the age of 5 it was getting very difficult and took a great deal of time and energy, but finally I made it and just as I reached up to grab the toy... My Teacher, Mrs. Rappe came in and snapped at me. It scared me to death, she smacked my hand and told to go back to my mat. I wanted her to put me back, but she said "You got off the mat, and You can get back on the mat"!

I did and I never got off the mat again during rest period!

Dreams Do Come True!

§

Mrs. Blythe's back and side yard was like a park. She had swings sets, a jungle gym, merry-go-rounds, and any other toy a kid would want to play on.

Everyone's favorite was the big tree, but of course I never could climb the tree. Mrs. Blythe and the other teachers would put me on the swings or the merry-go-round or in the sand box, but "teachers didn't climb trees", so the tree was out.

One day I was looking up at the big tree, wishing... when my Dad came to get me.

I told him about the tree, and he asked me if I wanted to go up... I nodded my head yes!

He scooped me up and we started climbing. It was so *scary*, but so *great*!

After that day, I always knew... I could do anything!

What's in a Name?

❦

Tracy 1967

The kindergarten was arranged with 4 class-rooms, with a teacher in each room and every so often the children rotated so sooner or later they all had each teacher. One time we had a new teacher, her name was Mrs. White. When I was rotated to Mrs. White's class, I didn't know her name. The first day, we played a game to learn all the colors. All the children held a card naming the different colors, and one kid would read another kids card and that kid would read another etc. I remember sitting in the circle looking around and seeing which cards I knew. I thought I knew them all except one, and I wasn't too sure about another card... "yellow". I just hoped she wouldn't pick the one I didn't know, but sure enough she picked "that one". I looked at it real hard and finally said "I didn't know it" and she said "of course you know this one", but again, I had to say... "I don't know". I really felt bad, because all the other kids were watching me, but then the teacher said "you know it, its the same as my name", but I didn't, because I didn't know the teachers name. I looked at the card real hard, but I still didn't know it, so finally I had to tell her, "I just don't know". She then said, "White... Mrs. White". I was so embarrassed, and after that day, I never forgot her name again!

16 Years of Dreaming

❧

Most kids can't wait until they turn 16, so they can drive. I was no different... except I did not want to drive a car... I want to drive an electric wheelchair.

When I was five years old, I saw my first electric wheelchair on TV, and I wanted one. I asked my parents and they said when I turned Sixteen, they would buy me one.

When it was nearing my 16th birthday, I started getting really excited, but by this time my disease had progressed quite a bit, and my parents did not think I was able to sit up to drive. (They did not tell me of course, but I overheard them talking).

They decided to take me over to a friend's house to try their electric wheelchair, just to prove to me that I could not do it, and that would be that!

That made me more determined than ever. I didn't tell them what I had heard, I decided to just show them!

We went over to the Goodsons, they had 3 boys in electric wheelchairs, and when we arrived, Dad

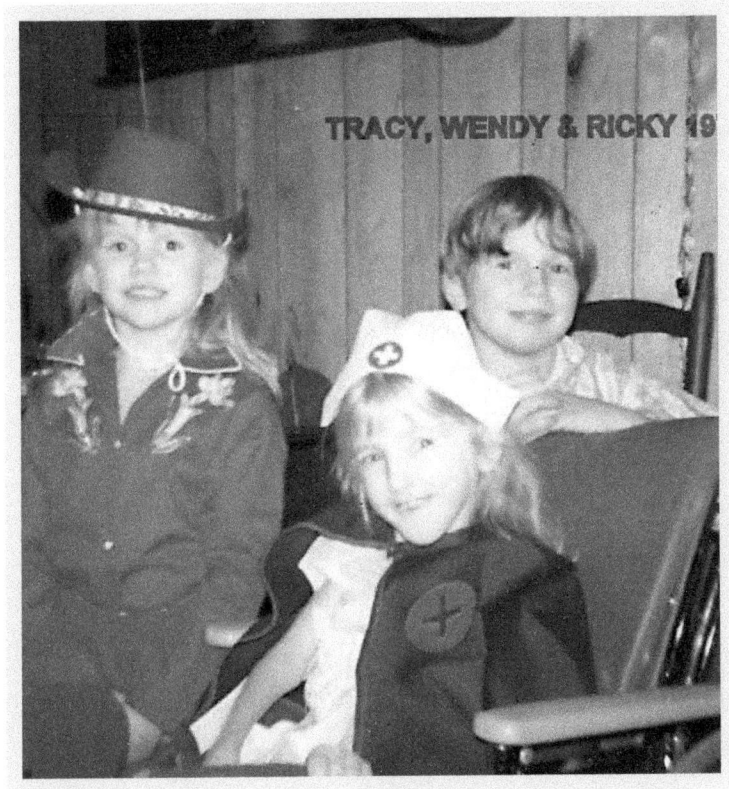

TRACY, WENDY & RICKY 19'

strapped me in. I was too short so they put a pillow under me and strapped me up again, and what do you know... I DID IT!

I started zooming around the room through the kitchen and around tables and anywhere I could go.

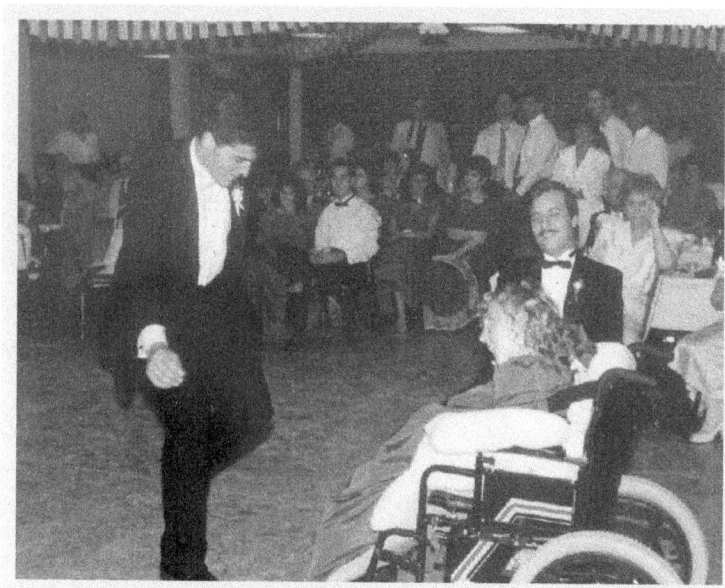

My mom just sat on the couch with her mouth open saying, "I can't believe it, she is doing it"! The tears weren't far behind.

"A Tree Fell On Me"!

§

One Sunday afternoon, my parents, brother, sister and I all went to the movies and then to dinner.

We went to the cafeteria next to the movie theater so we wouldn't have to load and unload my wheelchair.

My wheelchair would not go through the line, so Dad put me at a table while they went through the line.

I felt a little awkward sitting there at that large table all by myself. As I sat there, one of the waitress's came over and started to talking to me. Even though I was only 10 years old, she talked to me like I was a 3 or 4 year old, but I was pretty used to that. When she got ready to leave me she gave me a big hand full of change. I tried to tell her she didn't need too, but she insisted, so I gave up and just said "Thank you"!

I watched the waitress as she went over to another table to pour them some tea, and they started talking, I knew they were talking about me... I sure was wishing my family would hurry back...

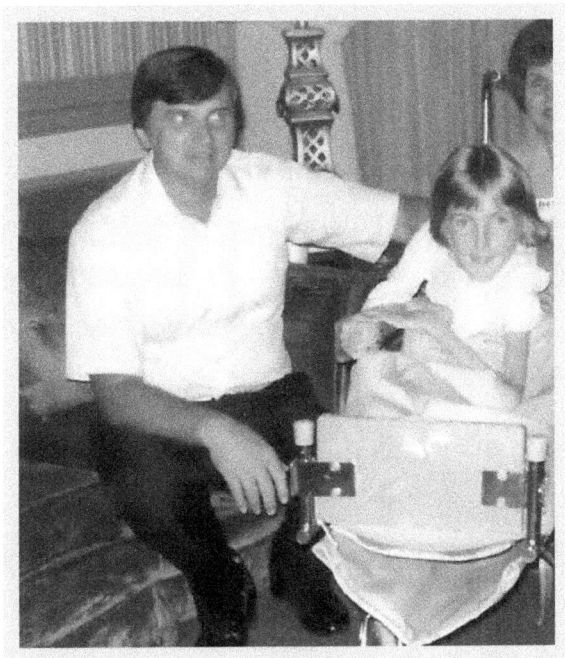

I could see that everyone the waitress went too, they were talking about me, and then as each of the tables were ready to leave, they would come by my table and give me money.

When my family returned to the table they asked me where all the money had come from. I told them, and they started laughing and making jokes. Dad and Mom said they should have dropped me off an hour earlier and I could have paid for dinner!

Just as we started eating, the waitress came over and started talking to my Mother. She asked what was wrong with me? Mom said "She has Infantile Progressive Spinal Muscular Atrophy Werdnig Hoffmann Disease", the waitress just looked at Mom totally confused. It was obvious she didn't know what in the world Mom had just said, but after a long pause the Waitress finally said, "Oh yes".

When she had left, we all decided that from that time on, we would just say, "Oh, a Tree Fell on Her" (and that was the beginning of the tree story).

Sunshine

§

TRACY WITH BROTHER RICKY

Not too long ago, I was in bed asleep. When I woke up, I started calling Frances *(Tracy's caregiver for ten years)* to come upstairs and get me up.

Sunshine, my cat was asleep on my feet, had awaken and came up and laid on my stomach, punching around to get comfortable. I said good-morning to her and started yelling again.

All of a sudden, Sunshine jumped up, ran up onto my chest and started kissing my face. It was like she was telling me "It's okay, I am here", then she went back and laid down on my stomach again.

I decided to try again, so I let out another big yell "Frances", Sunshine leaped to my face and started licking me cheek and ears. "No sunshine, that tickles, stop", I said. Finally she went back and laid down. I thought now what do I do? I waited a minute or two and tried again to get Francis's attention. But this time instead of going to my face she went to my arm that was sticking out of the covers and put her teeth around my arm, like she was saying "I'm here, what more can I do? So if you don't hush, I am going to bite you"...

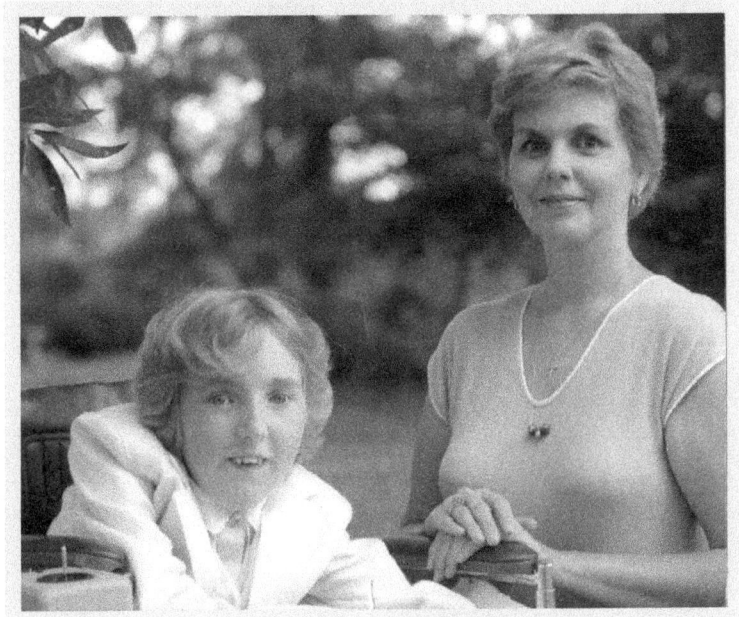

Now what do I do? If I yell, she'll bit me, and If I don't, I will be in bed forever!

Just then, I thought I heard Frances so I yelled one more time. Sunshine stretched out her paw, and put it on my hand... tensing her nails, not to hurt me, just sort of a warning...

Thank Goodness Frances heard me, she came to the foot of the steps and called... "Tracy, is that you?" I said in a very low voice... "Yes, Help! I am being Captive".

Whoever said that cats were dumb animals? Sunshine knew I needed help and she did what she could, what more could a person want?????

My Other Family

§

Dr. McLean * Guppie * Presbyterian Hospital

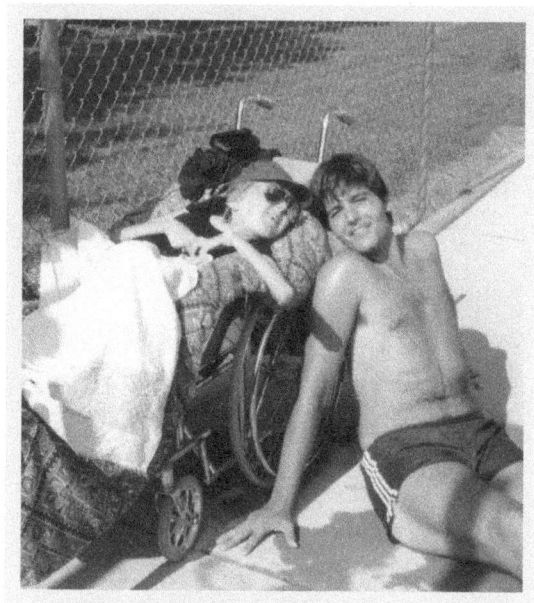

I have spent a great deal of my life in the hospital. When I was younger, I went in every two to four weeks, sometimes even more. I guess you could say it was my second home!

But it wasn't all that bad, as most of you probably think. I got a lot out of it... First of all, I received a great education. How many kids know what a "cc" is? How many five year olds know the difference between a "Suction Machine" and an "Ivac Machine"... and know how to operate both of them? In fact, how many adults know for that matter?

...And then there were all the great people I have met. Let me start with my family, I don't mean my blood family... I mean my hospital family. I know I cannot mention everyone. I don't have enough time or paper, but spending as much time as I have in the hospital... I guess you could say I have met a great deal of the hospital staff, from the Maids to the President of the hospital... from the Dietitian to the x-ray Technician and so many others.

I must tell you about Mrs. Gupton, or "Guppie" as I know her by. When I was little, I couldn't say "Gupton" so I just called her "Guppie" and it has stuck to this very day.

Guppie was the Director of Pediatrics, and I say "was" because she retired on March 7, 1986 after 24 years. A great loss for pediatrics and for all the people who will go there in the future.

Guppie is so full of love and caring, that as soon as you meet her, one feels a special bond. She was not only there to help the patients, she helped the entire family. On more than one occasion she was there when my Mother needed a shoulder to cry on, or to put Mom to bed in an extra room, when she refused to leave me.

When no one else could get my "IV" in, they would call "Guppie" and ninety percent of the time she got it in. Even when she couldn't get it in... it was okay... I knew she tried her best and it hurt her as much or more then it hurt me.

You know, I believe all of my nurses feel something special for me, and I know how special they are too me. Not just any nurse I may have, I mean "My Nurses".

I have known some of them since they were in nursing school and have seen them get married, have children, and grandchildren. I have met a lot of "My Nurses" families either at the hospital annual Christmas party, or the shopping malls around town. They are all apart of my family.

When I was little, the day after I was admitted to the hospital, I was able to (as we call it) "run the halls". I used to love to "run the halls"!... and as soon as they would let me out of bed... I was in the hall.

I spend a lot of time at the nurses desk. All the nurses would talk to me and let me help them do whatever they were doing. I would help fold diapers, write on thermometer envelopes, or help get the medicines ready and then we would go around and give out all the medicine. My nurse friends even made me a little nursing hat and name tag, so I could pretend I was a real nurse.

Dr. McLean

ᛦ

R McLEAN
1970

And now for **"My Doctor"**... Dr. McLean is the greatest doctor in the world... well I may be a little prejudice because we have more then a doctor patient relationship. I care for him very deeply!

How many doctors do you know that would go to your confirmation, or to your 16th birthday party or just call you up on the phone to kid you or to see how you are doing? He is a doctor where it **counts**! He has pulled me through a lot of bad times, when all the other doctors had given up on me, Dr. McLean wouldn't. He kept trying new things, never giving up and if he had any doubts, he never let it show to me or my parents. He not only is a doctor, but he is my friend and he loves me.

There are more then doctors and nurses in a hospital, so much more…

Mrs. McBain is the teacher at Presbyterian Hospital. Just because you are in the hospital doesn't mean you get out of doing your school work.

Mrs. McBain has never actually taught me, because I was either too sick, or I would get well and go home. But I do know her very well.

I will never forget the time that Mrs. McBain came to me with a problem. She was suppose to teach a boy how to do his Algebra. The problem was she did not know how to do the chapter he was on... so she came to me. We spent the next hour going over the chapter so she could go teach the boy that afternoon. What a switch, the teacher being taught by the student! And she brightens up all the rooms she enters with her books and "love".

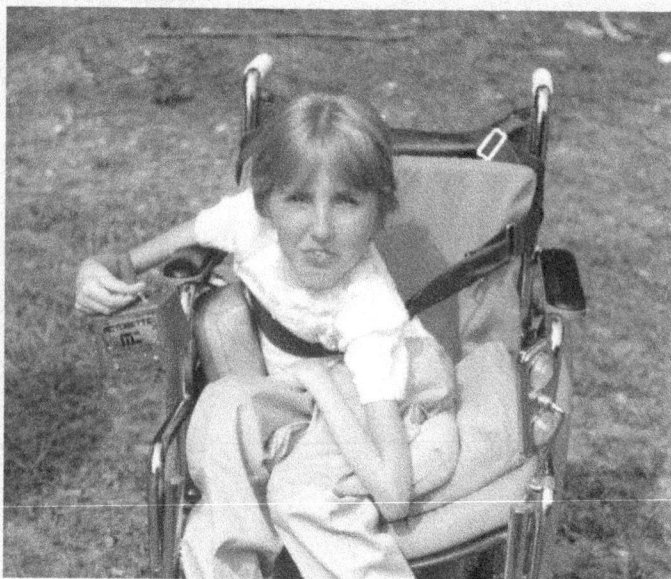

And let's not forget Sandra Smith. She is the Play Room Lady. Sandra has only been at the hospital a few years, but she has already become a major part of my family!

She is so nice and full of love! I so look forward to seeing her whenever I go into the hospital, it almost makes it worth going.

And the thing is, I know she really cares. Last summer I got pretty sick. I was having a lot of trouble breathing, so they were going to put me in ICU. I was pretty scared, too, and had not slept in 4 nights, because every time I would doze off, I would wake up gasping for breath, so I wouldn't sleep. Besides being scared, I was exhausted.

When Sandra came in that morning she came straight to my room, and we told here where I was being moved to. I was trying not to show how scared I was, but I could not stop the tears. I never could, I can stop myself from crying, but the tears come no matter what I do. But it was okay, because when Sandra heard what was going on, her tears began also.

She kept a check on me all day, and when she finally had to leave she gave me her home phone number and told me if I needed something or just wanted to talk to call her. That meant so much to me.

Since then she has come to the hospital on her day off just to see me, and she also came to my home on Christmas Eve, and so much more. But that is the way she is! I am not just a job to her, I am her friend!

Tracy* Roger Price

❦

And then there are all the patients and their families. There have been a lot of them through the years, but the kids we have known best are no longer with us.

Kids with so called "Terminal Diseases" have a tough time, because they not only have to deal with their disease but with their feelings about their parents and families.

Dealing with your emotions about your parents is the hardest part of having a terminal disease. I guess it is because with the disease there isn't much you can do about it, and you know in your heart it isn't your fault. But with your parents, you know if you were not in the hospital or sick, they would not be going through this. Ninety percent of the kids I have known with terminal disease, including myself think more about what their parents are going through or will be going through when what... even more concern then we are about ourselves.

I know for myself, I worry about their lack of sleep, or their emotional state. Whether it is being upset about how sick I am, or what the nurses are doing to me, or knowing that my parents are fight-

ing between themselves because of all the tension and lack of sleep due to my illness.

I remember this boy when I was little... Roger Price. We spend a lot of time together in the hospital. He was there because he had cancer of the lymph nodes.

Since we were in the hospital so much together, we became very good friends. We would go to each other's room and play games, or color, or just watch TV and Talk.

TK & TRACY HAVING SLEEP OVER AT TK'S HOUSE

When Roger was feeling okay, he would push me up and down the hallways. I remember once, Roger and I were bored, so we got on the elevator and rode up and down. We wouldn't get off because we were afraid we'd get caught. We had already been warned not to get on the elevators, but we were always doing something mischievous.

Our friendship went past the hospital, we would go to each other's house and our families would get together and have Bar-B-Q.

I remember one such Bar-B-Q, all of us kids were playing in the backyard until dinner was ready. Roger really loved squirt guns, and he had a lot of unique ones. We were playing with them until dinner, but there were not enough to go around, so Roger went back in the house and soon returned with a shoe box full of syringes. They were prefect as squirt guns. He had all sizes, from the really little ones, like a diabetic would use, to the jumbo size, that looked like they were made for an elephant.

As we started to fill the syringes with water, one of the kids from the neighborhood exclaimed that we shouldn't play with syringes. He thought they were gross to play with. We didn't think they were gross! I guess kids that spend a lot of time in the hospital play with different toys than other kids.

Although I only knew Roger for two years before he died, he made a great impression on me, and I have a special place in my heart with his name on it.

My family is still good friends with Roger's parents, Alma and Al Price.

During the time Roger and I were becoming friends, our Mothers were becoming friends too. Because Roger and I were so sick, our Mothers spent a lot of time together helping each other through times of crisis.

Mom* Dad* Ricky* Wendy* Tracy

§

Tracy with Mom &Dad

Mom

I can remember so many times when Mom would spend hours talking with a mother or both parents that had a sick child in the hospital. I guess because Mom had been through so much with me that she could relate to what they were going through, and she knows what they need to hear.

My Mother knows a great deal about all different kinds of diseases and their treatments, although she has not learned these things from books. She knows a lot just from all of her experiences at the hospital, and sometimes this is just as important if not more important when dealing with parents.

My nurses must know this to be true, because I can remember on more then one occasion, when one of my nurses would come and get Mom in the middle of the night because a parent needed someone to talk too. Mom was there with the right words to calm them down and hope to lift their spirits, and with a shoulder to cry on.

Death (Croaking...)
God's Promise...

§

As you can see, I have gained a great deal from the hospital, but I have gained so much more then I can ever put into words. I have learned so much about life and death, and what they are both about, and how to deal with both.

As for life, I believe you should live one day at a time. If you try to live in the future, you will never find happiness, because you will be too busy worrying about what is or what may happen to enjoy what is happening right now.

The same with the past... you cannot get the most out of life if you are not in the present.

As far as death goes... dying is part of living. I can't understand why people are so afraid of death. Just the word "Death", or "Dying" scares people too "Death".

I am not saying I don't have any fears about the subject, because I do. I am not afraid of dying... Just what may lead up to dying. I have been around death all of my life and that is scary.

Another reason I am not afraid of dying is because of my faith. I know I am going to heaven.
How do I know... because God promised this, and
in heaven there will not be any more pain or un-
happiness... so why should I be afraid?

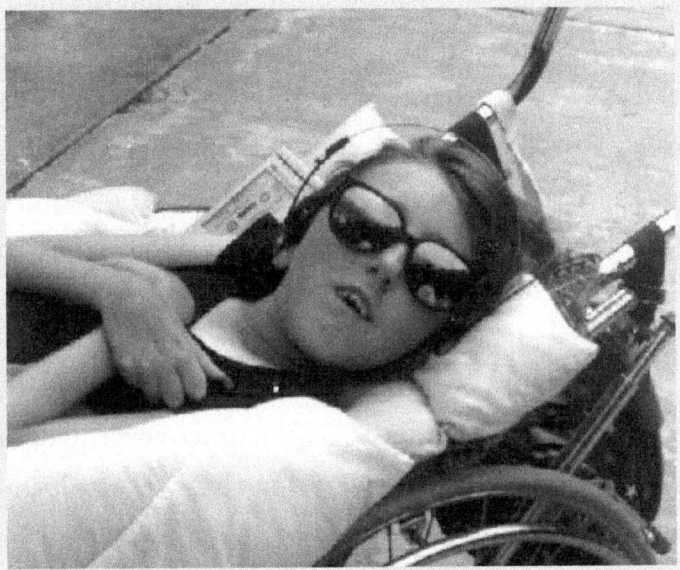

Mom and I spent a lot of time together when she wasn't at work, but I remember one summer she left her job to spend the summer at home. We had so much fun. Every morning we went outside to the pool and stayed outside all day long, eating breakfast and lunch outside. Mom hooked up a fan to keep the flies off me when I wasn't in the water. We really got tanned that summer.

We would decide who we wanted to invite for lunch and then we would plan our lunch menu and late at night, the night before whoever it was we invited... we would stay up late to prepare the lunch menu. I read the recipe and she prepared the food, and then the food had to pass my "Seal of Approval"... which means... if I liked the food... I tasted the food.

During that summer, my friend Suzanne Stevenson and Keith from WBTV came over and spend the day doing an interview for the MDA telethon. We invited some of my friends over for a pool party... Carol and Jerry and my Camp attendant. It was a long day of filming and talking but I am pretty used to it by now, this makes the third special film they did on me and its always fun to be with Suzanne and Keith (the cameraman) plus my other friends. The film got pretty deep, they interviewed us together and we went through an entire day in my life then they interviewed Mom alone and myself alone and that's when it got deep... but if the film can help someone... then what was said is what should have been said.

Suzanne hosts our Telethon and she's the greatest, she always rubs me to bring her good luck and she is a person who really believes in what she does. I really love Suzanne and she loves me. We have a great friendship. Keith, I have known for a long time. He does all our telethons and he is great! He always has something funny to say, plus you can tell he is all heart! I always look forward to seeing them both, they brighten my day in so many ways.

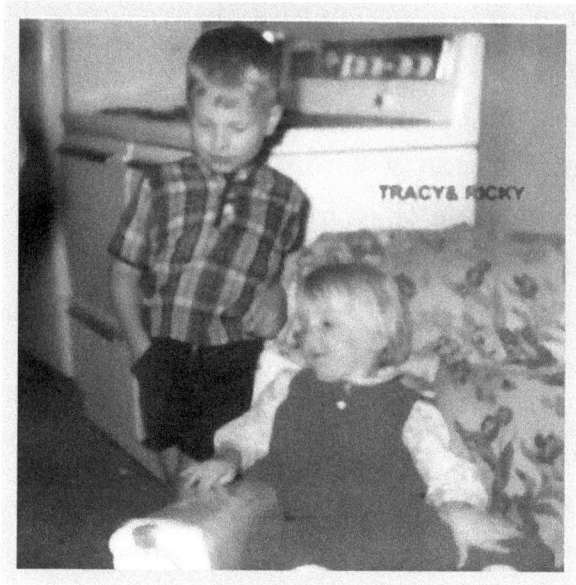

TRACY& RICKY

I remember when I was little, my brother Ricky, would sneak into my room and wake me up (everyone else was asleep). He would carry me downstairs to the pool table room and we would get under the pool table and play... play... play. Sometimes when he carried me down two flights of steps it would be pretty scary, but knowing how much fun we would have made it all worth it. Sometimes we would get up in the middle of the night and play. If we got tired, Ricky would put me back to bed and he would to to bed and Mom and Dad never knew we had been up and playing.

66

Ricky married Tammy, she is a really nice girl and we have become close over the years. We can talk about anything and she is a good friend. She isn't scared to pick me up or anything. We do a lot of things together and she comes over to visit me and even took me to her parents house to visit. Tammy is full of love and kindness to everyone. I have gained another sister, my family keeps growing.

My sister Wendy and I have had a lot of fun too, we go shopping, to the movies. Mom gives us so much money to buy an Easter dress or School Clothes and we go to South Park and look in every store until we find just what we want. Then Wendy flirts with the boys. We always see people we know so it takes us a long time to shop, cause we stop and talk to everyone.

I finally made it to "Aunthood", Wendy and Keith had a baby girl on Christmas Eve. We had our regular "Open House" and Mom and Dad were going all around excited about the new baby, I was just as excited. Me, an aunt! My niece's name is Sky, and when Wendy came home from the hospital, she came over here to stay and my Aunt Kathy and Uncle Danny and Cousin Sherrie came from Maryland to see the baby. We had such a good time. Dad bought a movie camera, just to take movies of Sky. He gave her a bath and it was so funny... he washed her face like a car... Mom was excited and I just laid on the couch laughing. I couldn't see what was going on in the kitchen, but I could imagine from the sounds in the kitchen. You learn to listen and you can know a lot of things that are going on by just listening.

Aunt Kathy and Mom played a joke on Wendy and Keith. They went to their house to get some more clothes and Aunt Kathy and Mom took blue eye shadow and put on Sky's face. They didn't say a word when Wendy and Keith came back home, but Wendy went to get Sky as soon as she got back and all of a sudden she looked down at the baby and

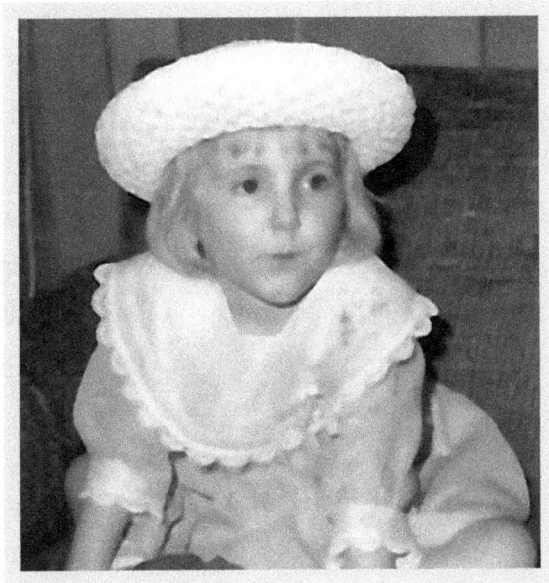

got all upset wanting to know what happen to the baby. Mom and Kathy told her they were pitching her back and forth and Mom missed catching her and she went behind the couch... Kathy threw too hard... I was really laughing inside, because Wendy really believed them. She started crying and Mom felt sorry for her and told her they were just joking and she said no they weren't, the baby was blue all over, it took them a long time to convince her it was only blue eye shadow. Sometimes it gets crazy in our house!

I remember all the summer vacations we took, and still take. We usually go to the beach for a week and have so much fun. Wendy, Ricky, and I plan a show for one night and we do a show for Mom and Dad, and we always take someone with us on vacation, so there is usually a crowd. We can stay up real late and go to the stores by ourselves and we always go to Myrtle Beach to ride the rides one night.

We went to Sunset Beach several summers and rented a house, we usually went with another family. This one time, we arrived and Mom and Dad were unpacking the car. Ricky had his fishing pole with him and threw it into the water without any bate and he started yelling he hooked something... no one paid any attention, since we just arrived and they knew he didn't have even a worm on the pole... well, he did caught something—a fish—and we cooked the fish and each got a little bite. Ricky was so proud of his fish, he thought it was the biggest fish there was, but really it was not that big, but I wouldn't tell him any different, cause it made him so happy.

One summer we went to Florida to Disney World, I know that was the hottest I have ever been. We just wanted to stay in the pool. Mom and Dad wanted to go eat good food and we wanted junk food, so most every night, they would go to a restaurant and we would go to Pizza Hut or McDonalds. It was really fun to eat by ourselves, then we could stay up late and watch TV and play cards.

One time we went to the mountains and we went to a park with the biggest sliding board I had ever seen. I wanted to go down it because Ricky and Wendy were going down it, and they were having so much fun. Mom didn't think I should, but Dad said he would take me. Mom got so scared, she had to walk away and we went up and down a bunch of times. Dad always made sure I did everything anyone else would do. Mom gets scared sometimes and Dad has to take over and tell her to walk away. I always tell Mom she raised me to do everything and there isn't anything I can't do... then she gets scared over high things but that's because she is afraid of height. I am happy Dad isn't!

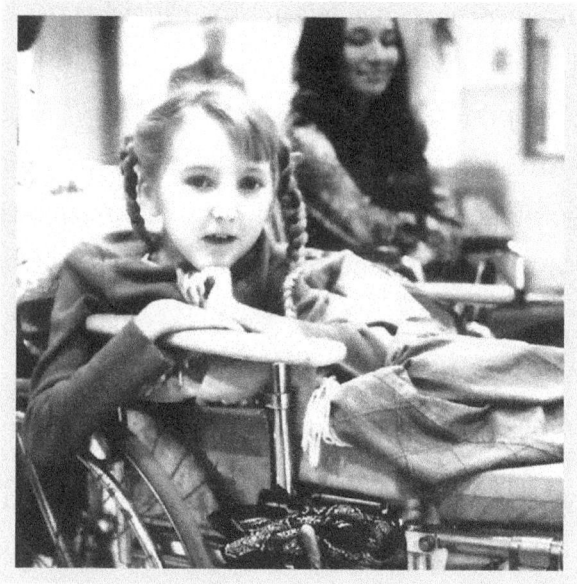

We do everything that any other families would do, and we take the wheelchair everywhere! Mom and Dad would say "what's a few steps"... and off we go... sometimes it got pretty scary but it was exciting too.

"Truly" my friend… Zack

A lot of people know and have faith, but they are still afraid, like my friend Zack. When we first met, we had a lot of trouble because of this subject...

I have this habit... have not decided weather it is a good habit or a bad habit yet... but it is the habit of... making cracks when people are scared or nervous. Cracks normally eases the tension, so when someone is afraid to pick me up or move me, I just say "Don't worry, it won't Kill me" or if someone is afraid to let me do something... like ride a roller coaster, I would say "I've done it before and I haven't died yet".

Whenever I said anything like this to Zack, he would get very upset. He didn't want me to talk about death, so I tried my best not to say those things in front of him... but every once in a while... I would slip, and he would give me a dirty look.

Zack had never been around death. He had never had anyone close to him die. They always say that people fear the unknown, and that is certainly true in this case.

About a year and a half into our friendship, a good friend of ours died. His real name was Lynn Arrowood, but everyone called him "Catfish".

His death hit me real hard. First of all I would miss him real bad. I always looked forward to the days I would see Catfish, he always had a joke to tell. Most of them were pretty silly but they would always make me smile. Second, I guess it hit a little too close to home. Catfish went through a lot before he died, and I guess I was afraid that I would someday have to go through what he did. That is still a very good possibility.

Catfish's death hit Zack pretty hard also. He finally could not ignore death, he had to think about it.

Zack and I went to the funeral together. Zack's brother George and My sister Wendy also went with us. On the way to the funeral, I found out this would be Zack's first funeral. Sitting on his lap, I could feel how tense he was. I wanted to make him feel better, but I didn't know how, so I just told him what would be happening.

This funeral was different than any I have ever been to. There were a lot of people yelling praise the Lord, and gospel singing. One man even went hysterical and fell to the floor and had to be carried out.

During the homily, I leaned up and whispered in Zack's ear, and asked him if he would be one of my pall bearers? Zack did not like this at all! He gave me a look that could kill and told me to shut up!

It was 2 am a few weeks later, Zack and I were sitting on my front porch. It was a beautiful night.

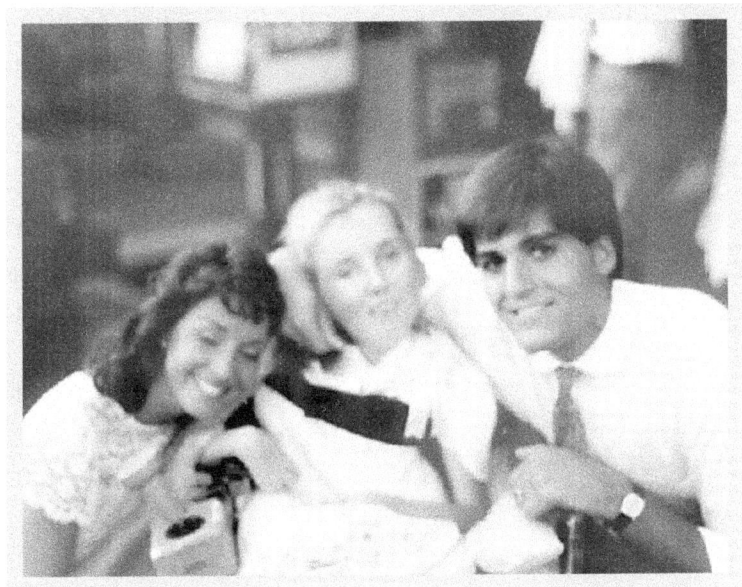

The moon was full and bright, and the air was crisp, but I was not cold sitting in Zack's lap. Sitting on Zacks lap was the perfect place to talk and talk we did for a couple of hours!

One of the major subjects was death and dying. We finally got it all out in the open, no more dirty looks, no more having to watch what I say. By the end of our talk, Zack and I had an understanding. Zack wanted me from then on to talk to him about anything... including death.

I believe that by talking about it, Zack became more at ease, because after that, it never bothered Zack when I made a crack about dying. A few weeks later, I even caught Zack making a crack about me croaking... We both grew a lot that night and our friendship continues today. We have a bond of true feelings and openness that only few ever have in a life time.

Soul Friends

Maria * Carol * Diane * Phyllis

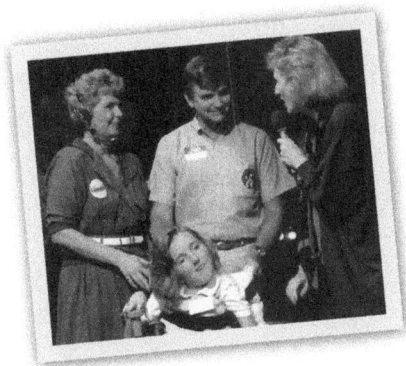

There are so many funny stories to tell about, but typing is getting harder each day, and it takes me so long to write a page. Mom said I should tape my thoughts. I think I will start doing that, I really get tired now and have a lot of trouble breathing.

Maria and Diane and I have really become soul friends and we go out a lot together or just over to Diane's house and talk for hours. Maria is going back to Florida soon and I will miss her so much. Seems like all my friends are moving away and here I am. Somedays I feel so depressed, but I don't want to worry Mom and Dad, I can tell time is short for me and I really am beginning to feel so tired. Lately, I feel like something heavy is sitting on my chest and its so hard to breath and it scares me when I can't breath. I am so tired... I have tired to tell Maria time is short, I can tell, and I just don't want to fight it anymore, but I want to know everyone will be okay. I am trying to wing Mom and Dad, that's a hard job... they are so tired... and I am so tired...

Notes from Tracy's Mom...

Tracy had many more thoughts; some I found on little cards, written in tiny handwriting, some I found in her note pads, in her wallet and her safety lock box, and Francis (Tracy's caregiver for 10 years) gave me some tapes she had made her last days here on earth.

Tracy loved everyone and accepted everyone where they were... she taught me so much, and now, almost seven years later, I can finally gather all her things together and put it in a book she started. I have added some of her poems, pictures, and newspaper articles.

I will always miss Tracy, her fight for life, and how brave she was in life... All the wonderful people we met because of her have truly left their mark on me as a person.

Losing a child is the hardest path I have ever walked in my life, but she left me with many riches of wisdom which I can hopefully pass on. The best part is knowing that I will see her again one day and she won't be in a wheelchair or hurting... This God has promised, and, like Tracy, I also have the faith of a child.

To those of you who were close to Tracy, thank you for loving her and giving so much of yourself to all of us.

God truly places children where they should be, and I end this with a poem by Erma Bombeck a friend gave me many years ago:

Most women become mothers by accident, some by choice, a few by social pressures and a couple by habit.

This year nearly 100,000 women will become mothers of handicapped children.

Did you ever wonder how mothers of handicapped children are chosen?

Somehow I visualize God hovering over earth selecting His Instruments for propagation with great care and deliberation. As He observes, He instructs His angels to make notes in a giant ledger.

"Johnson, Beth, son. Patron saint, Matthew.

"Forrest, Marjorie, daughter. Patron saint, Cecelia.

"Rutledge, Carrie, twins. Patron saint… give her Gerald. He's used to profanity."

Finally, He passes a name to an angel and smiles, "Give her a handicapped child."

The angel is curious, "Why this one, God? She's so happy."

"Exactly," smiles God. "Could I give a handicapped child a mother who does not know laughter? That would be cruel."

"But has she patience?" asks the angel.

"I don't want her to have too much patience or she will drown in a sea of self-pity and despair. Once the shock and resentment wears off, she'll handle it.

"I watched her today. She has that feeling of self and independence that is so rare and so necessary in a mother. You see, the child I'm going to give her has her own world. She has to make her live in her world, and that's not going to be easy."

"But, Lord, I don't think she even has a strong enough faith."

God smiles. "No matter. I can fix that. This one is perfect. She has just enough selfishness."

The angel gasps, "Selfishness? Is that a virtue?"

God nods. "If she can't separate herself from the child occasionally, she'll never survive. Yes, here is a woman whom I will bless with a child less than perfect. She doesn't realize it yet, but she is to be envied. She will never take for granted a 'spoken word' or a child 'sitting up.' She will never consider a 'step' ordinary. When her child says 'Momma' for the firs time and rolls across the floor, she will be present at a miracle and know it! When she gives this child hope, she will see it as few people ever see it in my creations.

"I will permit her to see clearly the things I see... ignorance, cruelty, prejudice... and allow her to rise above them. She will never be alone. I will be at her side every minute of every day of her life because she is doing my work as surely as she is here by my side."

"And what about her patron saint?" asks the angel, her pen poised in the air.

"God smiles. "A mirror will suffice."

(Adapted from *The Special Mother* by Erma Bombeck)

TRACY

Do you remember asking me once "if I was a vegetable, what kind of vegetable would I be?" I have thought and thought about this ever since you asked me, and I couldn't come up with an answer to this, except for a "squash, it looks just like me", but you said "No", that was my *body*, not me.

Well last night you said something that has been nagging at me ever since, but I finally figured out what it is. I am not a vegetable at all, I am a tree. It doesn't matter what kind of a tree, just an ordinary little tree.

Let me tell you about this tree... To all the people who go by it looks like a nice little tree, leaves, branches, and so forth. It blooms when it is suppose to and everyone thinks it is a happy tree, but if you look closely you would see that the tree has root rot, and there has been a hard freeze, and some of it's branches had frozen and died, and will never grow leaves again, and a woodpecker had been pecking a hole in the top of the tree for some time. It had gotten very big and is getting bigger and deeper every day. I don't know why this tree is still standing. There is no logical reason why... Maybe it is partly because the little tree knew that when it falls it will crush everything surrounding it. This little tree loved and cared about all the houses, trees, and others plants around it and does not want to crush them. But, sooner or later the tree must fall. It is inevitable. Maybe if a gardener would come alone and take care of it, water it, fertilize it and just love it, it could live a little longer, but no gardener wants to waste his time and energy on this tree, because it will never be anything but what it is... a sick little tree. So the little tree just stands there waiting, and waiting, and waiting... As the tree waits it hopes and prays that a nice friendly lumberjack would come along and chop it down, and put it out of its misery. The tree knows it will still crush something, but if the lumberjack chops it down, he will make sure it will fall in the right direction to crush as little as possible. The longer the tree waits the more spread out the branches will be

and the more things will be in its path and crushed.
So what do you think?

Your soul friend Tracy
4/16/86

(This was written by Tracy after a conversation
with her best friends, Maria and Diane, who read
this at Tracy's funeral)

Poems to My Best Friends
(Zack, Maria, and Diana)

I have a friend out there
She is full of love and care
Even though I don't see her every day
I understand and its okay!
Because when I hear her voice on the phone
My heart is lifted up upon a throne
We have been special friends since the day we met
I couldn't have found a better one, you can bet
Her name is engraved in my heart
And I know her love will never depart
Her body leaves from time to time
But her love remains, ringing like a chime
What more is there to say
Except that I love her more every day

§ § §

So your Birthday is here again
And here is the prize you win
Another year with me as a Friend
But when it is over that will not end
Because I want more then a year
It feels so good when you are near

Well maybe I got the prize
Because you are so wise
You always know the right thing to say
And in just the right way
I wouldn't trade you for a million
I might think about it for a billion
Well "Happy Birthday" to you
Have a great time in whatever you do!

§ § §

A chill goes over me as I think of you
I feel the tears swell up in my eyes
As I try to fight them off
But it is no use as they come rolling
Out and Down my Cheek every time
Your name enters my mind
And that is constantly, every time I hear
A Song, Every time I see a Rainbow,
Every time I see anything.

§ § §

Just because you are there
That's why I care
It doesn't take much to be a friend
Just to know when I call you will be on the other End
And every once in a while
Pick up the Phone and Dial
Just to Know you Care, and Love me
That's what makes me, a We.

§ § §

Are you studying hard?
Or are you sitting on you lard
Yes I do mean you buns
I am just having a little fun
I know that MCAT is suppose to be tough
But you really know your stuff
So it should be a breeze
But it wouldn't hurt to get on your knees
But I have Faith in You
Because you don't just have one head, you have two
Yes, I mean yours and mine
So you'll be just fine
Well, Good Luck on your Test
I know you will do your Best.
Your voice is a ray of Sun Light
It makes the droopiest flowers Bloom
And the Rainiest Days bright
The sound of your Voice carries me through the
Days and the Nights
and give me Hope for Tomorrow

§ § §

Happiness Is:

The sound of a friend's Voice
A warm hand in yours
A gentle Touch
A Warm body lying in bed next to you
Someone to say "I Love You"

❧ ❧ ❧

Friends:

Some Want to be Friends with their Mother
Some Want to be friends with Their Lovers
Some Want to be Friends with Their Friend
But First you Must be a Friend with yourself

❧ ❧ ❧

How Bright Will This Day Be?

How Bright Will This Day Be?
Life is like a Rainbow
Some days are as Bright as the Brightest yellows
And Some are So Blue
Some are as Hot as the Hottest Reds
And Some are the Coolest Green
Some are as Tangy as an Orange
And Some are as bitter as Purple
And when you put them all together you have Life!

§ § §

My Days Grow Dark
Since you have Departed
My only glimpse of Light is When
I hear your voice over the miles
of Wire that stretch between us,
or when I hear your footsteps
Approaching in the distance
When you put the Two of Us
Together We create Something
Beautiful, Like a Rainbow, So
Bright, So colorful, So Wonderful,
But So Unique

Tracy Lynn Armstrong
May 25, 1964—October 19, 1989

A Mother's Cry

I remember the day she was born...
I planned her future just to form...

Oh, how I loved this child of mine...
Never knowing what the end would find...

Then it came the day we were told Tracy would die...
I searched for an answer, I told them they lied...

From Doctor to Doctor I did search...
But all the answers were just like the first...

Oh God, help me to be Brave and Strong...
This I prayed during the night so long...

Our little one would become so sick...
"Call the Clinic" I would yell in a fit...

A Calm voice would answer the phone...
Then I began with all my moans...

This is how it all began...
Six Years ago upon God's Command...

Each day she is dying just a little bit more...
For she grows weaker and prays to the Lord...

Her Body is like a pretzel...
But God made Her "Special"...

I know she is preparing her way to go home...
But Oh! Will I miss her for so Very Long...

(written by Tracy's mom, Janice, during a long night at the hospital as Tracy struggled to breathe)

Memories of Tracy

Tracy Armstrong

It is harder to say who Tracy was to me than it is to describe the impact she has made on my life. Without a doubt, she has single handedly helped build my "half glass full" lens I stare out at the world with every day. She also made a significant impact on the eternal flow of optimism and positive attitude I carry with me every moment that I must. In addition, I attribute my abilities that allowed me to contribute in corporate America as a Human Resource generalist to Tracy and the infinite amounts of sensitivity, compassion and integrity she exemplified during our time together. As an owner of a home healthcare agency today, my competence and reflexes to act in the most care-giving manner are in part due to the many life experiences I shared being with Tracy. This would make her my life coach, motivator, teacher, and mentor. She also played the role of an accompanying angel, a bright light, a comforting hand, and a gentle wind. She was a bridesmaid, a fun road trip partner, a best friend, a person with a disability, a beautiful woman, and an incredible human being, to mention a few.

I never have seen tears of sadness in her eyes unless it was for a dear friend who passed away, unfortunately a common occurrence when you belong in the muscular dystrophy family. Never did I witness self-pity or anger for what God has dealt her. There were the few occasional scoldings I would receive for arriving "Greek time" (late) for our dates or when I acted foolishly trying to embarrass her. And the one time she narrowed her eyelids and tightened her lips was when we watched the MDA telethon from her hospital room and Jerry Lewis expressed concern about his critics and how they were trying to minimize the tremendous efforts of the MDA.

The dignity she carried broadly on her shoulders was evident whenever the muscular dystrophy family was involved. As a lifeguard at the MDA summer camp pool on my first night, Tracy in our very first true interaction, proudly and reverently spoke about the campers I will meet, the parents who needed the break, the camps that run across the country, the big brothers and sisters who volunteer, and the disease that will someday get a cure. She shared this with me so that I do not dare go another moment in my summer camp duties without understanding and appreciating why I was doing what I volunteered to do.

Humility and compassion came easy to her—like there was no other way to act regardless of the situation. After one of her many trips to the hospital where she would be given emergency IV because she had become dehydrated (a mysterious and common side effect of her disease), I walked up to her room to find her bed empty. The nurse took me down to the cancer ward where terminally ill children were being cared for. Through a glass, I watched Tracy in the middle of four young children, no hair on their heads and no color in their skin. They were smiling, laughing, and forgetting about their own misfortunes as they stared at Tracy, listening to her stories and answering their questions. She caught my glance and winked at me as if I caught her in a secret. On another hospital stay, a man walked into Tracy's room and asked her permission to bring his little girl who had multiple sclerosis to visit with her. He had heard about Tracy even from his daughter's hospital room three floors up. Tracy smiled at him with her big blue eyes and responded with sincerity, "Who, me?! Why, of course!"

As much as I felt she was truly an angel, divine and dreamlike, I saw the mortal side peek through from time to time which made her that much more lovable and credible. After being sung her favorite song "Truly" by Lionel Riche himself under a spotlight on a stage in front of thousands of fans, she was in a cloudy daze that lasted for a few hours, not unlike the same shock I am sure young women felt when going to a Beatles concert. My friends who joined us for dinner after the concert were enamored with Tracy's "stars in her eyes", a testimony that to my friends, Tracy always seemed so herculean.

Her patience and ability to understand others helped her deal with people day to day... people who would stare, cry, or even get angry at God when they would meet her and see the physical effects of her disease. Tracy's first introduction to the elders of the Greek community in

Charlotte came when we went to the annual Greek festival. At one point, she was surrounded in her "limousine wheelchair" by a group of older Greek women, all crying out emotionally and spitting on her "shooing away the devil and evil spirits who did this to her". Tracy smiled at them, thanking them, and even telling them not to worry at all as one of them pinned the "evil eye" to her headrest and patted her face. She told them all that she is in good hands because she has found her Greek god, and she rolled her big blues over to me. The women would then smile, wiping their tears on their aprons, and laying plates of Greek goodies at her feet whispering to me that she needs to be "fattened up".

My lowest moment in my 48 years of life must have been the day that, after receiving my eighth or so rejection letter from another medical school, I realized that my lifelong dream of being a pediatrician was for the time being not within reach. I was extremely depressed and embarrassed. Tracy called me and talked me into going out for drinks. Sitting in our favorite bar for over four hours, Tracy allowed me to vent all my frustrations, anger, sadness and fears. I cried for the first time in front of anyone. Though she did not have the ability to wrap her arms around me, I felt her embrace, her compassion, her love and her sensitivity. She also gave it to me straight—suck it up, re-think your goals and how you will achieve them, and get right back on the saddle. She made me promise her that I will always find work that I care about, be happy with, and work hard in. Do these things and success will follow. She also reminded me that I still had to fulfill my promise of buying her a Toyota van when I hit it big (doctor or not)! We laughed the rest of the night. And I never got depressed ever again. Though I never became a doctor, I did buy a Toyota Previa van years later. Tracy was not around to ride in but I did laugh every time I drove it and thought about that memorable "pep talk".

In that same bar, where we had many many conversations that brought us closer than anything I had experienced up to that point, I learned a few "life lessons". Tracy taught me to open up, to say "I love you" when you felt it, and to become more self aware. Tracy also helped me understand that death, like birth, was part of life. Tracy knew I was not comfortable talking about death, about anything being terminal. She had a way to bring it up indirectly and make it light enough in bite size portions to prepare me for the inevitable. She turned to me one night, while she was sipping on her coke and rum (sorry Mom, we did sneak a few here and there!) and I was on my third beer, and asked me when I get married, would I include her in my bridal party. I did not blink—of course. She is my best friend, and regardless of who I marry, she will be a bridesmaid. She smiled with satisfaction, not knowing I had taken the bait. She then asked, "That is good to know, because I want you to be my pall bearer. Will you?" I got mad at her for talking like that, got up and paced the room, and then sat back down in front of her. The whole time, she stared at me with her baby blue eyes, alternating a grin with a "forgive me" smile, but nevertheless, waiting patiently for my response. A few nights later, when I was kissing her good night leaving her house, she asked me again but this time she said "You are my best friend. You know the likelihood of my dying is greater than I getting married. Either way, I want you to be there. I need to know you will be there for me like I will always be there for you." Tracy was one of 10 bridesmaids in our wedding. I was one of six pall bearers in her funeral. As she taught me, best friends do this for each other.

Showing respect to someone is more than just lip service, a very important life lesson I learned from Tracy. Shortly after meeting Tracy and spending some time with her, we took a road trip to Chapel Hill to visit a friend. We had gone out that evening to a bar and enjoyed a night of drinks, music and dancing. About an hour after we got home that night, we had to rush to the emergency room when Tracy became de-hydrated (unfortunate side effect of her disease). I was very frightened and unsure of what to do. Her mother convinced me that this was part of her disease, she has been through this before, and not to worry. Twenty-four hours later, Tracy was discharged and feeling fine. A few weeks later, after another evening of going out, the same thing happened. And a few months later, for the third time, we found ourselves rushing to the hospital for an emergency IV. I became concerned that our evening out was causing her to dehydrate and subsequently need to go to the emergency room. Because the first couple of hours in the ER seemed like excruciating pain for Tracy (picture trying to put an IV in an arm or big toe where veins were too thin to find), I was determined in not having Tracy experience that again.

Therefore, I informed Tracy that we are not to go out to bars anymore. She was saddened by my comments and though she understood, she did ask me to reconsider. She explained to me that if it was not an inconvenience, she really appreciated the opportunity to go out and enjoy some social life even if it meant that she would have to "pay a price" for it. I was nervous, but agreed to it, not realizing that deep down in my subconscious I had made the decision not to go out again. After a few months went by, and I made excuses about not being able to go out, Tracy finally had to approach me for the truth. When I told her that I could not put her through that pain again, she then explained to me once again, respectfully but with much more conviction this time, that this was her life, and it was her right to make choices and decisions, and to suffer or enjoy the consequences of those decisions, not unlike myself. That it was not fair for me to make those decisions for her. That if I respect our friendship, and her, that I would respect her decisions. My discomfort subsided and my respect for her grew. We went out that weekend—with no subsequent visit to the local hospital at least for that night!

As I became more active with the Muscular Dystrophy Association, I was selected to go to a national meeting of volunteers in Sedona, Arizona. Upon my return, I was asked to present to the MDA board and family members what I learned and what I planned to do in result of those learning's. Sitting in the back, waiting for my turn on the agenda, I was becoming very nervous about speaking in front of this group. My palms were sweaty, and I kept practicing what I was going to say in low whispers (obviously audible to those near by as they looked at me with curiosity). Tracy pulled up beside me in her electric chair out of nowhere and smiled at me. She introduced herself and then asked me who I was. She made me laugh as she politely made light of my situation and told me I had nothing to worry about—I was a good looking guy and that everyone would focus on that instead of what I had to say! I was called up to give my presentation and the whole time Tracy was smiling at me and making faces. The session went very well based on the questions, enthusiasm and the clapping! I was approached by a few on the board upon conclusion of the meeting and I did not get a chance to thank Tracy before she left. Who would know that a year later, I would meet her at summer camp and we would become best friends.

Zack, Tracy's best friend

§ § §

To a Special Angel from a Stranger:

God has blessed me with two wonderful neighbors and friends as well as the parents of Tracy Armstrong. I did not have the opportunity to meet this young lady they proudly call their daughter, but the one thing I do know is that Tracy is simply not a stranger in my life.

With laughter and tears, I have seen pictures, watched home videos, and heard many family stories shared by both her parents. Tracy's story is just amazing, admirable, and has impacted my life forever.

Tracy's life story exemplifies that in life or death, there is NO obstacle too big or small for one to overcome when you have strength, courage, perseverance, and faith. With the loss of both my grandmother and mother in the past year, Tracy's story is also the reminder I need that teaches in the midst of death there is reason to celebrate. I thank God for the ARMSTRONG family, their daughter "Tracy" and my unknown friend and special angel who I anxiously await to meet at Heaven's gates.

With Love,
Mary Ingram, unknown friend

§ § §

My heart is filled with joy and laughter when I think of the times I spent with Tracy. Always full of life and living it to the fullest of her abilities, she always dreamed of making the most of life while living with SMA. Tracy and I could relate on so many levels because we both shared life with SMA. We both chose not to let it control our lives, but we were out to control it with the best fight we could give. One of my fondest memories was swinging in a hammock, holding each other arm in arm while looking out over the ocean and sharing our dreams.

One thing about having a body without the use of muscles to hug a friend or family member, it gives you a greater desire to be able to express your feelings. It comes so natural with Tracy. All it takes is looking into her eyes. The hammock that special day gave Tracy and I the opportunity so desired between two friends to comfort each other, not only did we hold each other, we shared our dreams, we shared laughter and tears, feelings no one else could understand.

Without use of her muscles and ability to move only her hands and facial muscles, Tracy had the most electrifying gravitation that would pull you in and give you the desire to get to know her. I can still picture her eyebrows moving up and down as a sign of excitement as we planned some of our mischievous moves to capture another adventure. Everyone was drawn to Tracy for her strength, her caricature, maturity, and love of life, not physical weakness from SMA and being in a wheelchair. She was a comedian in her on rights. She loved to make people laugh. If you had a joke, she had a story to top it.

Tracy holds a Life degree in Psychology. It is amazing the strong abilities one achieves as a result of weakness in another area. Friends would confide in her or share a problem or heartbreak over a boyfriend and a mature answer for a solution or at least great advice on what to think about was given by Tracy. She was a comforting friend to many. I had the better of two friendships. One with Tracy and one with her parents Richard and Janice.

We also had a bond between our two families which gave us even more opportunities to share special times together. During the late 70's and 80's both families were strongly involved in the Muscular Dystrophy Association. This is when we first bonded and became friends. We also had the pleasure of getting to know other families and volunteers involved with MD. We were very active with the Jerry Lewis telethon and many wonderful times were shared with adventure. We planned trips to the beach for the group, which for many was their first time away from home. It was exciting as we worked to make dreams come true for others, which enriched our lives even more. It is amazing that many of the friendships have become everlasting as we remain in contact with so many still today.

I have so many wonderful memories, it is hard to narrow them down. I had the honor and pleasure of crowning Tracy the first Junior Miss Wheelchair North Carolina, a title that is given for one's Achievements. We both shared a love for music and dancing. If anyone dare question if a person who can not move their body has rhythm, all they would need to do is watch Tracy's eyes dance to the music. One other thing I noticed we had in common was always repeating two sets of words that were natural for us to use anytime we asked or needed help or felt that we were interrupting one's schedule—"Thank you" and "I am sorry".

I think of Tracy and her braveness in preparing others for her departure to Heaven. I only pray that I can be as brave. God has a plan for each and everyone. Tracy exemplified uncountable measures on earth and will forever touch the lives of those who had the honor of knowing her. One young lady accomplishing more than many put together. She did it with love, grace, dignity and admiration. My life will forever be enriched for the truest example of a friend, I can say, Tracy Armstrong. She will always live in our hearts until we join her in Heaven.

Robin Morgan Heffner, Mt Holly, NC

§ § §

I can remember getting to come over to Tracy's house often, our parents were best friends. At times when all the adults were outside, I would go inside to see what Tracy was doing. Girl time! We would sit and talk for a bit, then Tracy would ask if I wanted to play a game. Tracy had a computer game hooked to the TV. We each had joysticks for the game. Tracy had a joystick that was modified so it was a bit easier to manipulate.

Tracy would explain the game to me. She would so sweetly say, "All you have to do is circle all the objects that appear. Just don't touch the line to an object." Sounded so easy. HA!

I would get to go first. I think Tracy got a kick out of seeing how, um, well I did. It was the most difficult game to play for me. I would start to circle the objects and almost immediately touch the line to an object. UGH. Tracy's turn. Little did I know that my turn wouldn't come for a long time. Tracy has such great fine motor skills that she could circle hundreds of objects without the line touching any of them. I think when Tracy did touch a line she was feeling sorry for me having to sit there for such a long time. Tracy would look at me and just laugh.

Good times!

Margie Bazluki, Monroe, NC

§ § §

Every time I hear the song, "If you want to sing out, sing out," by Cat Stevens, it takes me back to the warm summer of Camp Bethelwood. That is where I learned the most about myself and others. One of my teachers was a young lady named Tracy Armstrong. I am sure she didn't consider herself a teacher to any of us, but we learned so much from her.

This special camp was full of courage and infectious spirits of young people who were trapped in a body that would not allow them to physically express their dreams and desires in the same manner as the average kids. At first you might have had the impression that this made them "less than" the other kids. Tracy quickly showed me, by example, that these kids were more than likely "better than" the other kids.

Tracy taught me that the most important part of the human anatomy wasn't your legs or arms, but your heart and what is inside of it. When your body doesn't do the things you want it to and you rely on others to help you accomplish various tasks throughout the day—you tend to develop special relationships with others that the independent person will not.

I have never met another person who was so determined to live life to the fullest, even with the most tremendous roadblocks placed in ones path, as Tracy. She was truly an inspiration to many who witnessed her in this pursuit. She always exceeded everyone's expectation.

110

I can only imagine how much she has accomplished since she left her physical body and is now floating above us all. I am sure she is still reaching out and touching hearts and minds. Giving comfort and courage to those who need it and sharing in the joy of those she loved and touched.

Jim Bazluki, Cary, NC

§ § §

To know Tracy was to love her. She truly was one of the most inspirational people I have ever met. She never complained about her disabilities. She made the best of what she had.

She was one of the most thankful people I ever met. No matter what you did for her she always said thank you. I remember her lying in a hospital bed so weak but still would muster up the strength to tell the nurses thank you. To top it off, she would smile as she said it.

She taught me to see the best in everything in life. Looking at her life, having spent 25 years in a wheelchair, she held her head up high and made a wonderful life for herself.

The last year of her life she wanted to go to the beach and see the sunrise over the ocean. In August of 1989, we went down to Myrtle Beach, SC. It was Tracy, Richard, and me. On the way down to the beach Richard got pulled over for speeding. He told Tracy and me not to tell Janice. However, Tracy could not wait to tell on him, and it was so funny. We got to spend a couple of days at the beach. Tracy and I got up early one morning and watched the sunrise over the ocean. It was one of those picture-perfect sunrise mornings. I am so thankful for that time we had had at the beach and for watching the sunrise. There was nothing better than just talking to Tracy for hours.

I also have so many memories of the MDA telethons. Before I met Tracy, I would watch the telethons and it would be touching; however, after I met Tracy and got to see the day-to-day struggles of living with MDA, it changed my outlook on this disease. There are so many people who are affected by this terrible disease. As I got involved with the telethons, I got to meet so many precious people that have been affected by MDA. We have got to find a cure...

Tracy always inspired me to be the best I could be. I had always wanted to be a nurse, and after meeting Tracy, I knew that I had to fulfill that dream.

Tracy also loved rainbows. I always think of her when I see one. You can look in the sky sometimes and the sky will be lit up with this beautiful rainbow. That is how my life was with Tracy; she brought so much laughter, happiness, and life into my life that I will never forget her.

Tracy knew death was going to happen. She planned her funeral. She wanted it to be a celebration of her life. At the end of her funeral everyone went outside. There were thousands of balloons all colors of the rainbow. The balloons were let go at the same time. It was a wonderful sight to see the balloons going up at the same time. I knew Tracy was smiling!!!

There is no way how to describe how special Tracy is that one would truly understand. I love you so much, Tracy, and can't wait until I see you again in Heaven.

Tammy, Midland, NC

Tracy never let her struggles and disabilities stop her from anything; what a wonderful and strong person she was. You always treated her as you did your other children and never made her feel like she was different. I remember when we thought that she would only be with us for about six years and how God kept her on this earth until she was 25 so that she could witness and deliver the word of God to others. What a blessing she was to so many.

Ann Crawford, VA

We thank God for our memories of Tracy. She made us all better persons in one way or another and taught us life's lessons that no book could ever match. There have been several times when Tracy's name, courage, and adventures have been shared with my friends up here in Canada.

Bessie Christophilakis, Canada

We met the Armstrong family when Tracy was 5 years. Little did we know what would transpire in the next 20 years. What a blessing it has been. Tracy touched all our lives by the way she lived her life. She was funny, smart, witty, and truly an example for all of us to follow. She loved life with a joy that only a special little angel could. She was truly a gift from God.

Tracy accepted the life she was given; if only we could all do the same. Love you, Tracy!

Mel & Arlene Hostetter, Leesburg, FL

§ § §

One of the most memorable moments with my niece, Tracy, was when our family and my sister's family went to Myrtle Beach, SC, for vacation together. The children, Tracy, Wendy, and my daughter Sheri, and Uncle Richard decided to walk to the end of the pier. Tracy was in her electric wheelchair, which was faster than us, but we all stayed with the pace. We were there for awhile, when Richard had to go back to the condo. He told us to stay on the pier until he returned. Well, of course, when we decided it was time to do something else, where was Richard? Nowhere to be found. After waiting and trying to decide what else to do on the pier, we decided we needed to go to the front of the pier to see what else was going on at the beach.

Tracy could always come up with something funny. Of course, being the adult and the responsible one, I should have not listened, but her ideas were always great and sounded like a lot of fun. Before I knew it, I was sitting in her wheelchair holding my niece on my lap. Tracy controlled the speed, and she opened it up, and down the pier and down the hill we went, with the kids running with the chair. We were all laughing so hard as we hit the hill, and wouldn't you know who was walking up the hill— Tracy's father. As we flew by him, his mouth dropped open, his eyes became huge and he turned around and started running after us and was not too happy about what we did. We thought it was so much fun, and Richard made it that much more fun. When we were retelling our adventure to Janice, we all laughed so hard, and Richard made the story funnier chasing after us.

Tracy loved adventure, and she was the leader of the pack that day; with her sister and cousin and Dad chasing her, she felt like the story of the runaway train. We always laugh when we talk about our vacation together. We miss Tracy, but I know I have an angel looking over my family, and, of course, we have our wonderful memories.

Aunt Kathy, Maryland

§ § §

Where does one start when trying to describe what Tracy meant to me? I would have to correct the sentence and say what she *means* to me. It started a long time ago.

In 1981, I was working as a lifeguard at a Methodist camp. One of the weeks at the camp was devoted to Muscular Dystrophy. This is where I met Tracy. I will never forget that day. It was hot. I was opening the gate to the pool... ready for a new group of children to have fun in the water. I turned to see some children running, others coming via "piggyback" on friends but many children in wheelchairs heading towards the water. At that moment, I became scared. How was I going to keep these children safe in the water? It wasn't very long before that "fear" changed.

I was in the lifeguard stand when a young lady approached in a wheelchair and asked, "Who is in charge of the pool?" I responded, "I am." She then asked for the time. I told her it was 3:00. She then asked me, "When will the wine and cheese arrive?" I couldn't believe my ears. Here was a small girl (she looked to be 5 years old) asking for wine and cheese!! This was my introduction to Tracy! My shock must have been seen on my face because she laughed as her baby blue eyes sparkled. She was 18 years old. This was the start of a friendship that remains in my heart to this day. Oh, I feel that I must mention that the next year my mother (who didn't drink) brought Tracy wine and cheese in small tupperware containers to the pool!

Tracy's personality spread throughout a room whenever she entered it. She was contagious. We became best friends and would travel to see each other as frequently as we could. We shared everything. I was "TK"/ Tracey and she was "Kiddo" / Tracy.

"TNT"—together we were dynamite!

There was nothing that we couldn't / wouldn't do. We went dancing with Carolina Basketball players in Chapel Hill... A simple OJ and vodka would do (sorry, Mom). I would arrive late at night and pick Tracy up from her house. Sometimes she would know where we were going and other times she would not. We would go out romping in Richard's yellow Karmann Ghia or stay at home and play backgammon. It didn't matter as long as we were together. We would go to a basketball tournament where the people didn't speak English, to the mountains to have lunch by a waterfall, Carowinds, horseback riding and, yes, even to the hospital when Tracy got dehydrated and needed IV fluids. All were adventures that allowed us to share memories that will be cherished forever.

Our symbol (for lack of a better word) became the rainbow. We seemed to see them everywhere we went. "One day, we will meet at the end of the rainbow," she would say. Or... we would be driving—rather lost—and she would want to know if I was looking for the end of the rainbow! Tracy drew me a picture of a rainbow that went from her home to mine.

118

We would stay up all night talking, sharing our dreams, our fears, and our innermost feelings. Nothing can replace that. It is called unconditional love.

Tracy taught me to get to know a person from their heart, not their physical being. She taught me that God has a plan for everyone... we just have to listen. She believed that life was a gift and lived every day to the fullest. She loved to have fun, and her parents allowed that to happen. Now, as a parent, I admire Richard and Janice for being able to let Tracy grow as a teenager / young woman and not limit her activities in attempts to protect her. I think this also kept Janice and Richard young. They taught me about flogging... if anyone does not know what this is... please learn. It might seem silly but is really fun! We used to laugh watching Janice and Richard doing this!

One memory that I must mention was when Tracy told me that we were going to see a new movie that had come out. She had seen it but she didn't want me to see it without her. The movie was called "E.T." She sent me a news article, a post card that week and said it was a must see for us both. However, she did have one condition. I could not wear any mascara to the movie. Tracy loved to pick at me and told me that I would cry. I told her "no way," that it was a fictional movie! The bet was on! During the movie, Tracy sat with a friend, and at a certain point, she asked to sit with me. I knew she was up to her tricks... I was NOT going to cry. In this part of the movie, "ET" is getting ready to return to his ship and head home... he puts his finger on his friend's forehead and says, "I will be here." Tracy looks at me and said, "That's where I will be when I die." I lost it. I cried and cried. She laughed and laughed at me. She told me that she knew I would cry and she won the bet!! In my heart, I knew what she was saying... and now I feel it each and every day. It doesn't matter that we are not able to be together physically... we are still together in our hearts and will always remain so forever! One day, God willing, we will see each other again, both of us dancing, holding hands, and laughing. Until then, I feel her presence with me every day.

When I would get down, I remember her saying... "Stop complaining—do something about it." When I cried, she cried with me and would then say, "Enough... go forward and be happy." She was the best friend a person could have. She was truly a present from God. I am forever thankful.

Tracy told me that she wished for things before she died.

1. To know what it would be like for her legs to hurt from running versus what she felt daily—her legs felt like bees biting her constantly.

I know that she is now "Dancing on the Ceiling" and is pain-free. One day we will be together again, and we will dance "All Night Long!"

2. To know what it would be like to be kissed.

She was kissed by more people than anyone that I know. Good looking guys!! Oh, a gal should be so lucky!

3. To see a waterfall.

I knew this was one that I could handle! We drove to Brevard (where I attended college), and I got a friend of mine to pack us lunch and meet us at a waterfall. Tracy and I were in Richard's car. It was cold... but she was totally surprised! Needless to say, when we returned to Charlotte that night, we got totally lost!! This was not an uncommon thing for us! It was half the fun!

4. To have a real boyfriend

I know that Tracy lived through a relationship that I had with a friend. When our relationship ended, I couldn't bear to make her choose between us. I withdrew from communicating with Tracy in hopes that she and my friend would remain close. They did, and for that I am ever so thankful. Their relationship was the most important thing.

However, I knew in my heart our bond was / is always there.

I would like to say that Tracy was the bravest, smartest, funniest, most loving, forgiving friend that anyone could ever ask for. She gave and forgave. She loved and is loved by everyone that knew her.

I will end this by providing a letter that she typed to me on December 1, 1982.

It is only appropriate to send it back to her...

A FRIEND TO ME

Dear God, Thank you for my Friend Tracey (Tracy)...

Tracey's / Tracy's Friendship means more to me than I could ever put into words...

She is there, when I need her, if not in person, she is there in spirit...

and I am there when she needs me...

A Friend is someone I can talk too and share all my happy moments with...

As well as my sad moments... and I can share her happy and sad moments...

When we are together, we have so much fun... but we do not have to be doing something to have fun... Just being together gives me a happy and secure feeling... we do not have to say a word... just being together is enough.

Just knowing that she is my friend, gives me a warm feeling in my heart... But most of all... I LOVE HER AND SHE LOVES ME!!

*So, Thank you Dear God for a friend like Tracey /
Tracy. She is more than I could ever wish for...*

I miss you my dear friend.

I will see you soon, "Kiddo!!"

Seygapo, Tracey ('TK')

§ § §

I remember when Tracy was working on this book!!
I went over to her house and she was at the typewriter
with a pencil. She insisted on typing everything herself
one letter at a time. She had the teeniest hands and fingers all curled around the pencil and she used the eraser
to hit the keys. She was resourceful and determined. She
was sort of lying sideways by the computer, but she kept
on!

And what a writer Tracy was! I remember the newspaper did a story on what a math whiz she was, but
I knew her as a fabulous writer. She wrote an amazing
essay using a metaphor of nature's majestic oak tree as
a symbol of her own life. The tree was big and strong yet
had root rot and she was worried when it fell it would
crush those who loved it. That typewritten essay on two
pages stayed in my desk as a source of inspiration in all
my years at work. That was so like Tracy—to be more
worried about others than herself.

Tracy was also such a huge inspiration to other younger children living with muscular dystrophy—especially at summer camp. Her parents gave her the wings and freedom to enjoy that special place and she became one of the older campers... sharing and sharing.

Tracy was a deep thinker and deep talker... we preferred to talk about real things and she was that way with all her close friends. To this day I have a special connection with her that she honored me with. She gave me a gift. The night she died, she called me at home. She was in the hospital and I think she knew she might die. I asked her very directly, "Are you afraid?" And her strong yet teeny voice answered me, "I'm trying not to be." I was so touched that she called me and we could share that very real conversation. I always felt she gave me more than I gave her.

Love to you both!

Suzan Becker,
Former WSOC Anchor, Charlotte, NC

www.ingramcontent.com/pod-product-compliance
Lightning Source LLC
Chambersburg PA
CBHW030515100426

42813CB00001B/50